Echoes

and

Memories

and

Night
Air

Echoes
and
Memories
and
Night
Air

POETRY

Crystal Heidel

BYZANTIUM
Sky Press

Byzantium Sky Press
Ellendale, DE, 19941

ISBN 978-1-955872-16-4

Library of Congress Control Number: 2023905436

First Paperback Edition: November, 2016, as *Landslide*

Cover & Interior design by Crystal Heidel, Byzantium Sky Press

Manufactured in the United States of America

Cover Photograph of woman by Baraa Jalahej, edited, blended with stars image by Bryan Goff.

Interior Photographs:
Copyright © Crystal Heidel, author's private collection photographs:
pages 77, 78, 93, 97, and 108.

The rest of the Interior Photographs are from Unsplash.com and Pexels.com; photographers are listed below in no particular order: Casey Horner, Freestocks, Kayla Farmer, Mahdi Soheili, Shot by Cerqueira, Dirk Ribbler, Jared Rice, Marina Abrosimova, Silas Bausch, Tanya Pro, Aditya Vyas, Annie Spratt, Benjamin Balazs, Content Pixie, Guille Pozzi, Praveen Kumar Mathivanan, Priscilla du Preez, Trevor McKinnon, Vengadesh Sago, Brigitte Tohm, David Moum, Hikarinoshita Hikari, Lucas Sandor, Max van den Oetelaar, Pixabay, Simon Lee, Toa Heftiba, Zolton Casi, Jared Rice, Michael Olsen.

for the hopeless romantics

Echoes
and
Memories
and
Night
Air

GOLD

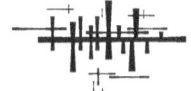

Billions of years ago, somewhere in our Milky Way Galaxy, a pair of neutron stars collided.

Neutron stars are the remnants of more massive stars that exploded into violent supernova. While their outer layers were expelled for light years into the vastness of space, gravity continued to press their dense core so tightly into itself that protons and electrons were forced together to make neutrons. They spin faster and faster and as they spin, they condense. Eventually these stars are so dense that the weight of a single sugar-cube sized portion of a neutron star is more than one billion tons.

A single sugar-cube. More than one billion tons.

My mind is amazed. I am in awe of this, our universe, and its ability to create and fold and condense and blast its way through the void of space. To take hydrogen and make helium and oxygen and carbon and nitrogen and make stars that shine and twinkle in the night sky, to let it simmer for billions of years only to explode into beautiful and spiraling gasses and dust that travels for light years. And it reminds me of writing and the constant wonder at where all my ideas come from. Where the energy, my "protons" and "electrons" of words, these simmering thoughts and stories and poems, come from.

The neutron stars generate elements higher on the periodic table than iron and nickel and when two of these stars collide, the ensuing collision creates the heavier elements of the Universe, including gold, platinum, and uranium. These heavy elements eventually coalesce into new planets.

I marvel at this. These elements were created in one of the most violent ways, yet what comes out of it, millions of years later, is truly beautiful.

Planets.

Worlds.

Life.

And what is more beautiful than creation?

Years and years of thinking and reading and absorbing life, of taking in everything that I learn, see, do, feel, touch, and experience coalesces inside me into a dense swirling, pulsating mass—a star of sorts. And just like two neutron stars rotating around each other, being drawn into the center of their mass, there is another pulsing "star" inside of me: desire. And when my first neutron star of compounded information collides with my star of desire, it causes an explosion of creation, in the form of thoughts and stories and characters.

This seems to happen over and over and over, almost daily. Like the Universe with matter, I seem to never run out of ideas. There is an abundance of them in me, like there is an abundance of gold in the Earth's core from those stars colliding billions of years ago.

The Earth's mass is approximately one-millionth gold, most of it being in the core. In fact, there is enough gold in the Earth's core to cover the entire surface of our planet knee-deep. Fissures in the Earth's crust from hot water when the planet formed created pockets of quartz and gold. And humans mine that gold today just as I mine for words and phrases in my writing. And just like machines digging into the Earth at depths of up to three miles, I dig into myself, searching for the perfect phrase, the best way to say what is on my mind or in my character's head.

Inside of me is a gold mine.

The Latin word for gold is *aurum*, meaning "shining dawn." It's a fitting definition since gold is the only metal that is naturally yellow. It neither crumbles nor tarnishes. In fact, there is an old Turkish proverb that says, *Gold does not rust on the ground and rocks don't get soaked in the rain.*

As a writer I find that there is always something inside of me—a poem, a story, a character—that I can write about. These things will not dissolve nor rust inside of me. They sit and wait until I'm ready. I may not use them for their original concept, but mold them into what I need when I get to that story or poem just as humans mold and transform the malleable gold into jewelry.

I have had an idea for a science fiction novel for the better part of ten years. I have been slowly planning and plotting, writing down character descriptions and history, giving life to what was once an idea. An idea came to me while I was paddle boarding one hot summer day. I was looking down into the water when a voice said, "There are some waters on my home world that are... what you would call purple." Though I knew this was a character, I still looked around, seeing no one. That was the main character who has transformed from a voice to a person with iridescent skin and a fascinating home planet entirely covered in water. There are others from that story that I have been listening to over the years, writing down their history, their language, their feelings. These characters have been patient with me, gently asking when their turn will be.

There is another story that has been brewing in me for several years. Not too long after the above idea came to me while paddle boarding, I was yet again paddling, and a character's thought popped into my head: *If I fall in, that will be trouble for this town.* And it caught me off guard. This turned out to be Caroline, a character I wrote a short story about in an anthology. I continue to jot down notes about her story, as well as the above scifi.

They are my gold, my ideas that are yellow in color and glow like that beautiful rock found in the ground. And they keep coming.

One question writers are asked all the time is, "Where do you get your ideas?" It's a question that most writers don't know how to answer because they don't know where they come from. They just *come.* These ideas and stories and things that need to be said come from within. From feelings, from heartbreak, from our past.

I like to believe that Jalel ad-Din Rumi, whom most will know better simply as Rumi, saw that inside of all of us is unnamed treasure, *a shining dawn* of unexpected creation. In one stanza in his poem titled, "We Can See the Truth in Your Eyes," he writes: *Why are you so enchanted by this world when a mine of gold lies within you? Open your eyes and come—Return to the root of the root of your own soul.*

Inside of me is a gold mine. A treasure of ideas just waiting to burst forth. Stories upon stories upon stories. They bubble up from little fissures inside of me, fissures made from colliding "stars" of information and desire. From this, I mine.

The Latin word for gold is *aurum*. On the periodic table, gold is abbreviated as Au.

Authors are also abbreviated as Au.

I'm an author.

I am gold.

PROLOGUE

Love is Not Logical

I don't believe in love,
or at least I don't think I do.
I believe in logic.
I believe in being rational,
and love is not rational.
It's not sane,
and it doesn't make sense
and it's not the fact that I have never loved,
for I have.
But it wasn't enough to call it real love.

It only takes a leap—
a word, a sentence, a laugh, a smile,
an understanding,
and I come undone.
Real love is like taking
    a desperate   last   leap.
It's as if tight-rope walking over
two buildings and knowing,
the only way down,
the only way to stop the feeling
    is to jump.
How many people take that leap?
How many people believe enough to let go
         and fall?

AUTUMN

Today the Sun is Shining on Nothing New

As I sit here
alone with my thoughts,
my memories of you are floating
like the bubbles in a glass of champagne.
They take me back to
that chilly twilight night
around a bonfire in someone's backyard.
I wonder if you remember that evening.
I was huddled under a flannel blanket,
red and yellow stripes as bright as the flames.
There were couples neither of us knew;
their conversations were a murmur.
We stood apart from them
taking in the sea of smoke and stars.
I wasn't sure what to say to you,
so I sighed.
You sipped your beer, glancing at me.
I saw you out of the corner of my eye.
Not quite sure what to make of me,
what to say to me.
I stepped closer . . . if that was possible.
But now my memories float
like those bright stars,
in that inky, cold sky,
and I'm afraid the sun is
growing tired of me.

Beautiful Mistakes

As soon as he left the room,
I felt my heart crumble,
or maybe it was just because of the empty days
and months that had passed already.
Seeing him again was reliving the melodic landscapes
that played over and over in my mind,
the images disjointed yet connected
by breaks and cracks,
empty blackness between,
like old nickelodeons.
They are a collision of swirling memories and
words left unspoken
from brief and dazzling moments.

Forgotten Things

I am the shot
someone else has bought for you,
the resulting empty glass
left at the bar as you walk away,
brown wood ringed with leftover whiskey.
I am the light between blinds,
stretching its fingers over the wrinkles of an unmade bed.
I am the stars in a constellation no one
gazes at anymore.
I am the last drop of wine in the bottle.
I am the bright crimson fallen leaf
in a puddle of mud and
the deep black of a new-moon night.
I'm the lost key in the back of a drawer,
or the one you find, but can't
find the lock it opens.
I am the dust on books you have never read.
I am the offerings at the center of a labyrinth.
I am these leftover things because I am
the chance you didn't take.

Heat

You skim my neck with your fingers.
I feel the heat of your hands,
a soft space of warm air at my neck,
only slightly warmer than your lips.
You scrape higher, move my hair,
send tremors down my spine.
Calloused fingers rough against my softness.
How can your fingers,
how can they . . .
I inhale sharply.
You groan against my skin,
and the vibrations are like the
taste of hot honey,
        sweet and sticky and spicy.

Your fingers slide down my arms,
pull me closer.
And closer, still.
I can't get close enough, I think.
And then I feel your breath against my breast.
I tremble.
Push me back,
pull me forward.
I can't think.

You, Only

You slam me against the wall,
hands grip mine before I can dig them
        into your hair.

Pushing hard, panting;
it's mine and yours—
it's soft and loud and synchronous.
Your fingers bind me.
Your hips anchor mine.
They make me want need hurt ache for you
and I want to say something, anything . . .
But I can only moan as your lips
contact my skin—
teeth scraping my neck,
burning lines.
Scarring me.
Your mouth presses to my ear.
Breath hot, hands fumbling.

We only want one thing.
I wrench free,
thrust my hands under your shirt
        and push up.

My fingers have a mind of their own
tracing the muscles of your arms.
A smile plays on my lips
I am desperate to explore.
Your hands drop lower,
slip beneath the silk fabric of my skirt
and caress me until I'm unable to stand.
I drop to my knees.
The button on your jeans—
        it must go.

Breathing Paradise

In every sharp inhale, I see you
struggling to maintain distance.
You push off from the table, putting
a few more inches between us.
I lean closer and take
a sip of your wine.
It dances on my tongue
leaving a sweet,
melancholy taste.
You lift a corner of your mouth.
My tongue swells, goes dry.
My throat collapses;
words leave my lips
but there is no sound.
Your eyes begin to glow, blurry, like
the sparks of dying embers
fanned back to life.

I should have listened to them.
I shouldn't have chased you.
I should have left that very moment
I saw you standing by the men's room door
willing to yank me inside and kiss me
absolutely
senseless.

You kicked the door shut, and
I giggled into your mouth when a woman
threatened to call the cops.
And then your lips captured mine again.
Yes, I do believe, paradise lies
beneath your breath.

He Doesn't Encourage Real Conversation

His language is unspoken
like a ship at sea.
Silent.
Far from land.
His language is in glances
hiding from the spray of salt.

In stolen embraces.
In smiles in dark corners.
In soft kisses.
In empty hallways.

His conversation is silent.
It's a secret he keeps.
I am his secret.

He doesn't let on,
doesn't even tell me
that the lines that tether his
thoughts to his mouth
are tight.

I Can't Help But Think This Way

It's my feelings he wants, my body.
The things I want,
those things deep down
I never wish to reveal,
the secrets I want no one to know,
he seems to know already.

I can tell by the way he curls his
fingers around the stem of a wine glass,
delicately, as if it were my throat.

It is in the way he knows my favorite red.
It is in the way he meets my eyes as he
polishes the glass.

I imagine him thumbing through
the pages of thoughts in my mind,
or searching an old card catalog,
pulling out specific likes and needs
and wants.

He cannot know everything, though,
he cannot see everything,
because tonight I tell him I want white
and his expression changes.

The Incident

It was a small incident and yet
I have often gone back to it in my mind,
tried to recall all the details.
I see the outline of your eyes
despite the deep shadows
in the corners of the room and
the absence of sounds in the restaurant.

> No clinking glasses or
> clattering silverware or
> plates crashing or
> rushing, frenzied servers.

There was silence that night.
A deep, never-ending silence,
heavy like the thick syrup of your voice,
heavy like the desperate words slipping off my tongue.
The honesty cuts
through the emptiness now.
And I wish I could take back those words,
        words I can't even remember.

Our Story

I could sense a downpour of sorts
under the clear sky tonight.
I had kept wishing for the outcome
to end differently,
but I can't see us happy.

In our story,
it's love ending in disaster.
We'll come up with a title
call it:
Never Should've Happened

I think we'll start with a chapter
about how we met.
Pages and pages, about how
you electrified my blood
      captivated
            thrilled and
                  chilled me.

And you can write about how much
you wanted not me
but the thought of me.
And how you thought
you could change me
into what your heart wanted.

As the plot thickens,
I realize,
I can't find my story's end
      in you.

Close to Invisible

I felt like a kid responding to a dare.
It had been in his eyes.
The remains of something we'd shared
once, long ago.
It had been our secret,
though it felt as if everyone knew.
He had stared at me,
his eyes ever roaming my face.
I had shifted
hoping it would move me
out of his sightline.
He changed chairs across the room.
Still, his eyes never left my face
    even when he spoke to others.

Now he's as close to invisible as
any man can get.
Though long gone from my heart,
his words echo between my ears,
like the thrum of hummingbirds,
and they bring an onslaught of memories.

Like how the dimness of any restaurant always
makes me look around for him,
      waiting
      for his arms to crush me.

Boxing Eyes

My eyes are puffy from crying,
as if I went ten rounds
with a boxing champ.
My body is shaking and it's
not from the whiskey that burned
down my throat,
splashing on an empty stomach.
Inside I am in turmoil
rocking and floating, wishing
I had never called,
never learned the truth.

NO is such a strong word
for being so simple.
No more long gazes
promising unspoken gifts of touch.
No more wondering if
that smile was more
than one given to a stranger.

INTERLUDE

More Like The Stars

Could there be any greater rush
than staring up into the midnight sky,
shoals of white-blue-yellow-pink stars
swirling across the Milky Way?

I wondered how—or if—I could only
choose one and love it fiercely.
Perhaps my wanting to find
only one star to illuminate my night
is foolish.
There are billions in our galaxy alone.

Perhaps my tendency to
fall hard
fall fast
and hit bottom before
I even know I'm falling
means I'm a meteorite
crashing through
the atmosphere
exploding over my horizon and
shattering into
a million sparks of fire
of different colors;
red and orange and green.
I can never gather those sparks,
or put them back inside me,
because they have burned out,
burned up,
in the atmosphere of my life.
They are part of my history.
Words and moments I cannot change
but the rush of speaking and living them
was worth the crash.

SPRING

You Are Dangerous To My Heart

You swallow up the current
and supercharge it.
Nerves flutter.
My body feels
like the gentle, rhythmic thrumming
of a bumble bee's wings.
About two hundred thirty beats per second.
Can you hear it?

Where The Stars Touch The Ocean

I thought we could go there
together,
that place Down Under
where our friend resides,
where the stars touch the ocean
and reflect impossible dreams.

I dreamt that we were there
you were grabbing my coat for me
because I was cold.
And our friend said, "You know
how to take care of her."

I woke with a start,
my skin freckled with gooseflesh
        my mind racing.
Did you know how to take care of me?

I hadn't taken notice of how many
times you had
but there it was.

I wonder now, what could have
happened if I had stayed.

Midnight Train

The night wraps me in a blanket of cold.
The snow falls in powder,
and like dust I have startled,
it darts left and right, searching for direction.

I am standing outside your door
waiting for you to answer,
like I am waiting
for a midnight train.
And I imagine I can hear the wheels
cracking on the tracks.
But in the fog around me?
Nothing.
No fall of your feet on the stairs,
on the creaking fifth step,
the one I skip when I leave.

Daylight is hours away
and I am longing for you,
for the whistle warning me,
for the way you stop and stare,
then smile and say nothing.

The snow turns heavy and
weighs my lashes
but I don't blink,
for fear you will disappear
that my train will never come.

My Harbor

My safe harbor is the crashing,
heavy waves and thick fog
between the rocky shore and the open sea.

A barrier of water,
so easy to slip through,
so easy to navigate.

But like that harbor,
you slip in and out of my life,
coming and going like ships at night.

If only I had an anchor,
or a dock that tethered you
between the rocky shore and the open sea.

Your Face I See In My Dreams

Though our time was short,
I would share a hundred more shots
of Țuică with you
if only to hear you say my name again.
And to wake next to you,
the sun through the window,
casting shadows on the eaves
above your bed.

Shells and Sand and Sea

I'll build our house of clear blue sky
with a pinkish-white sand carpet beneath our feet
so soft that I'll sink when I walk,
with palm tree fans overhead.

I'll use the short, lapsing waves as walls and
make a table from the shells at my feet.

There will be no empty place.
Rocks and stones will decorate the corners
and the sky might falter but will always return
as the roof, keeping me grounded.

I'd Do It All Again

The weekdays of fun and the tangled nights.
The conversations about the future.
Ours were skylights: little windows into the soul,
doors no one else could even
try to open.
Hemingway.
Shakespeare.
Our classics matched.
You introduced me to Casablanca;
it changed my life,
quickly became my favorite, too.
We talked hockey and watched tennis.
I told you, "I forgive you for
not liking football."

And I would do it all again,
just to see your face
the night she came over,
eyes wide, slippers on her feet,
rounding the corner of your condo
as we sat outside by the fire
that chilly April evening.
She said she came over the bridge
to see if you had seen the hockey game.
You watched her nervously—yet shocked.
I could see her wheels cranking.

When she finally left
we went inside and you locked the door.
You apologized and said you hadn't seen her in
over a year.

I smiled. "If you were anything for her like you
are for me, I can see why she came back."

Without Him

I tried for a minute not to hear those words
navigating through my brain.

He said he was watching his parents' house
while they were away in France.
Relaxing, he said, next to my Lucy.
My heart dropped.
My Lucy.
I was silent as images flooded my mind.
A laugh, Lucy is my dog.

I let out a breath I didn't know
I'd been holding.

I'll call you. I promise.

I remain silent.

I will call you.

I look out the window, to the westerly
trail of luminous red taillights.
Stars light the night now.
Only hours ago, alone, I had watched the
sky turn royal then black as the sun sank.
I had wanted him there.
I had wanted to show him the sky,
and say, *Look at that moon! Doesn't it glow?*

I'll call you. I will. Tomorrow. Count on it.

I think he is saying this more for himself
than for me.
It's like a mantra to him. If he says it enough,
he'll do it.

Okay. I close my eyes.

I know that the little amount of fear I feel
is going to be woven into the beauty of how
I'm meant to be.
Without him.

Bird on a Wire

I'm trying not to think about
the unresolved questions,
little locked rooms
in my heart.
My memories of the weeks
and the months gone by
seem to be in a foreign language.

I don't understand them.
Nor do I want to.
I don't want to remember
the late-night phone calls,
your voice
silk on my every thought.
I love your voice, still.
The tone.
The cadence.
The way you whisper your promises
so as to make me believe,
but you lie.

And your lies make me feel like a bird on a wire,
precariously perched so as not to get burned.
But burned I got and scarred I am
so take your lies and games and all the chances I'd given.
And take your Sorry's and all the plans you'd canceled.
I don't need them.

Four o'clock in the morning,
several drinks in,
our favorite song fading into the background.
Let's go upstairs.

I wish I could go back to that night and
stop myself.
I wish I could say,
Let me crash on the couch.

But your fingers curled in mine,
and I felt like a bird on a wire,
precariously perched, unsure what to do.
I moved one foot and
I got burned.

Proper Goodbye

The day I last heard from you, the sky
was a kaleidoscope of blues and whites, melting
into blacks and reds as the night emerged.

I rose that night, peered out my window,
wishing for undeliverable wishes,
like the beautiful swirl of snowflakes
in an early summer sky.

Later that week, I escaped to New York,
finding moments of emptiness
on Chinatown's streets,
slipping quietly by small stores filled
with Buddhas' serene faces.

I let my eyes rest on a glass teapot
in the window of a store with blue floors
and a pocket-size garden in the window display.

I found myself lost in a city that never sleeps,
feeling so broken and fragile.
It would be easier to imagine the city in a nuclear winter,
whites and grays and shades of muck from
taxis clogging the streets.
The city never sleeps.
So why should the feeling of sadness inside of me?

On Canal Street, Escaping You

The air is permeated with fish and
whatever the grates and sewers send up.
Street vendors—
carts full of purple grapes and light
green cucumbers and semi-ripe strawberries
and pink and green dragon fruits—
edge the sidewalks, hawking,
stepping in front of me.
          "You buy?"

Red lanterns dance in shop windows next to
headless, plucked ducks.
A cart selling sweet cakes.
Mini jade elephants
sit on tables just outside narrow stores
with black and white tile.
Blue and white vases prop doors.
Red and yellow draped canopies
with symbols and letters and
lines and dashes I don't know the meanings—
or names—of meld into a long,
blurring shimmer of heat above the bustling people.
I peek in a store on the left;
paper umbrellas, wooden handles poking from a barrel.
          No. I don't buy.

In the park several bands compete
to see who can out-tradition each other.
High-pitched words I don't understand
dissolve into the pings of drums and strings
that soften the cacophony.
A funeral supply store across the street
reminds me that our lives drift through a series of people
and eventually, they end.

3:41 A.M.
(an exercise in not using THE)

Concentrated white-yellow beams
splinter blinds.
Crevasses
offer no resistance,
create iron oxide shadows.

Night is a dreamscape
woven to a sound in my mind.
A curtain drawn open,
a life I could have led.
There but
only in snippets and flashes.
A story of its creation.

I watch wedges of light on carpet,
lines move as time
drifts.
Outside a goose
    —a single goose at 3:41—
makes a racket for five seconds
then, it is gone,
pulled by gravity or instinct
to wherever he needs to go.

I roll over,
belly to ceiling.
Along white plaster,
small geometric abstractions
form words and say things
I need to hear.

We Didn't Fit

I wake in your bed,
one Saturday in April
after a hockey game.
The lines and shadows across the ceiling
are a beautiful stain:
red and gold and blue and green.
It had been raining;
streaks of water
drizzle down the pane of glass to my left.

I don't like this setup, where you are closest
to the door and I am sleeping on the window side.
I don't have an escape.

There's warmth in your touch, though,
    and your fingers reach out,
        across the bed of white.
They find my wrist and lightly
spread out, you press your
hand into mine,
our fingers intertwine.

It was something I had wanted,
but now that I had it,
it felt wrong.
Your fingers were
too cold
too long
too elegant.
They didn't fit.
We didn't fit.

Replay

On most nights
when I can't sleep,
when the prayers and wishes I've
prayed and wished for never happen,
I do what I know I shouldn't,
what I've promised myself I would never do.
On most nights,
when I can't sleep,
I replay you.

I remember how I held back when you
first asked,
Would you like to go to dinner?
I remember I had wanted to say YES
but I didn't.
I don't hesitate when I replay you, though.
I say yes. And we go to Lupo di Mare.

When I replay you I see the doors,
the ones you were replacing in your home,
as if you were showing me
that you are useful,
that you can fix things.

And I didn't think anyone
could air guitar "It Ain't Over 'Till It's Over"
by Lenny Kravitz.
But I replay you, your nose crinkling as you
        mouth the words.

It was April, and the air so chilled
you lit the fireplace,
a blanket covering us both,
the *Royal Tenenbaums* playing,
a movie I still haven't finished
        because we never finished it.

I replay that look of disbelief you gave me over
the lid of the Casa DiLeo pizza box.
You didn't believe for one second
that I wasn't hungry anymore
and you gave me a third slice to prove it.

I replay that look of admiration on your face
when you show me your 70th-anniversary edition
of Casablanca.
"Best movie of all time," you say.

I replay your hugs, your grip so tight
as if you wanted to make sure I was real,
that I wasn't going anywhere.

But mostly, when I replay you,
I am the one leaving.
When I replay you,
you are left replaying me.

INTERLUDE

Don't Fade, Star

I want to wake up later,
be in a different story.
Perhaps a different universe,
a different Earth.
One where you don't exist.
Or one where I am stronger than I am now.
Perhaps in that other
universe, I won't feel love or lust or
       whatever this is.

Lately, I am lost.
I find myself staring at blank spaces
on the wall,
wishing they were deep, dark,
pulverized skies—
skies without stars.
Because I have stared and stared,
I've stared at that sky so long, focusing
on one star,
and all the rest
seem to have faded.
They lost their light and all
I can see as I gaze, unblinking,
is that one star
and this star is so far away,
       it's unattainable.

I fear that if I blink,
everything I see—
that star—
will be an illusion.

How do I ask the question I cannot
bring myself to ask?
Because right now I feel like
I'm holding broken glass.
I can't squeeze any tighter
because it will go deeper.
And I don't want to let go because those glass shards,
stuck in my hands,
with skin growing around them,
trapping the beautiful, damaged glassware,
reflecting my feelings,
and that black sky
and that star,
          are all I have left.

And holding them is better
than having undamaged skin.

WINTER

January 1, 2016

I love that you didn't take your red
jacket off during the movie.
First date.
First movie.
First of January.
I loved that you leaned close to whisper in my ear
about Chewbacca and Rey
and how this *Star Wars*
was just a rehash of *Episode Four.*
I love that even though you weren't
thrilled with *The Force Awakens*
you spent the money to see it again,
with me.

And you loved bar hopping.
"Drinks and apps, and on to the next," you said.
I love that you drove because I'm
not sure I could keep my mind focused
on the lights.
I love the scent of your cologne,
spice and musk.
And I loved how you introduced me
to your friends as Chrys
because my stomach flips a little when you
use that name—not Crystal.
I don't think I could ever be Crystal to you.

And I loved that at the end of the night
you offered your bed to me.
But mostly I love that you didn't hesitate
when I said, "You don't have to sleep on the couch.
Sleep in the bed."

Flashes of the Past

I sit on your couch,
on the broken side that won't extend without a wrench.
My morning cup of coffee
cannot warm the ice water in my veins.

I look ahead, at the television; it's not even on.
But I see coronas of white light on the wall,
as if our story were
photographs of war-torn countries,
glass and dilapidating rubble,
concrete powder and dust caking
windows, and if you look inside the buildings,
through the shattered panes you could see
all of my memories of you in snippets.

> *"I think I'd like to adopt. There's too many kids*
> *who don't have homes now." You sip wine and*
> *I'm nodding and smiling. "I absolutely agree.*
> *Adoption is what I'd do, too."*

In the streets are broken chairs,
strewn and upturned.

> *"Is that what you're angry about?"*

There are pieces of drawers,
handles crooked, or missing
as if they weren't supposed to be opened,
and they weren't.

> *"Yes." And I want to be snarky, and dig into the reason*
> *but there are some things that should never*
> *be repeated.*

Wires dangle from bombed-out rooms on second
and third and fourth stories,
empty square shells, foundation crumbling,
exposing the beds and journals
of those that had lived there, once.

Like us, tip-toeing around,
trying not to disturb the dust on the walls.

Sea of Whiskey

I want to swim in a sea of whiskey.
I want my demons to pull me down,
and drown the taste of your lips
from mine.
I want that whiskey to burn any trace of you
from my lungs.
I want my demons to swallow what's left of you,
in the hopes that I will forget.

Content

I had been content just tracing the lines
in your hands with my eyes as I had held them,
memorizing them so I could feel closer to you.

I had been content just being next to you,
as you slept. I didn't even need to look at you,
just listening to the sound of your inhales
and exhales had been peace.

I had been content just to stay in, cook dinner,
and watch movies, or *Treehouse Masters*, or
Diners, Drive-ins & Dives, and plan road trips
to places we'd never go,
and to just be in your company—moody or happy.

I had been content and that was my mistake.
I should have wanted more,
I should have told you things
I have never told anyone.

I had been content to let you take the lead
and in doing so,
I let you lead yourself out of my life.

Inked

You're written on my heart
in permanent ink.
The type of ink that fades
not in days or weeks or months or years,
but in millennia.
It's beautifully abstract,
a sort of calligraphy,
symbols and words and numbers.

The colors are blue
and entirely engulf my heart.
I guess the words are written so
only I can read them.
These stories and memories
create a moonscape
and I guess they react to you, their creator,
darkening, etching deeper.

My heart is a lover of darkness
and each evening, as the sun starts to set,
I feel that this ink,
a watermark on my soul,
will never fade.

Sunlight

As I watch planks of sunlight slant over
the plains and valleys of your back,
illuminating the crests,
defining the shadows,
I think to myself:
I may have made a mistake.
But before I can even contemplate
what that mistake might be—
for it has no solid definition—
I am immediately lost in this moment
in a sense of timelessness,
floating, as if
I am in blue, endless water
searching the ocean calmly
even though I have thousands of miles
yet to explore
and every freckle
every curve
every nook
is a new place in the world.

Breathing Together

If I could tell him
how I feel,
right now,
without feeling regret,
I would tell him that I miss
the feel of his breath on my skin,
how it rustled my hair in the dark,
sending tremors of warmth down my spine.
I counted his breaths as he slept;
how differently we
breathed the air between us.
His was faster and steady,
and mine yogic slow, irregular.
I miss how I tried but failed,
to keep tempo with his breath.
I would tell him
that it was the way he curled his face
into my neck, his beard
grazing my collarbone,
inhaling deeply,
his words on that heavy sigh
that he loved the scent of me.
I would tell him
that all of those moments
still make me happy.

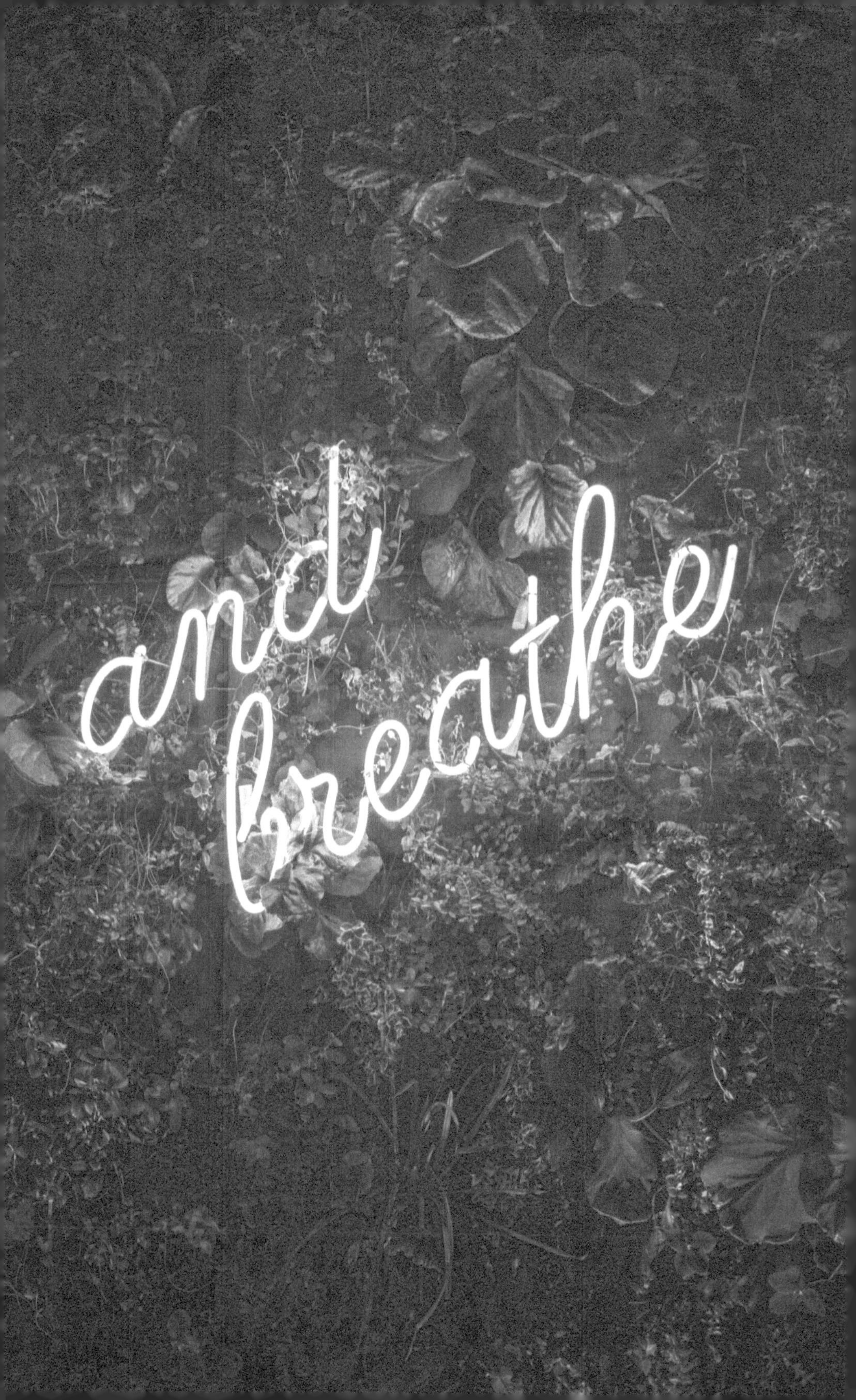
and breathe

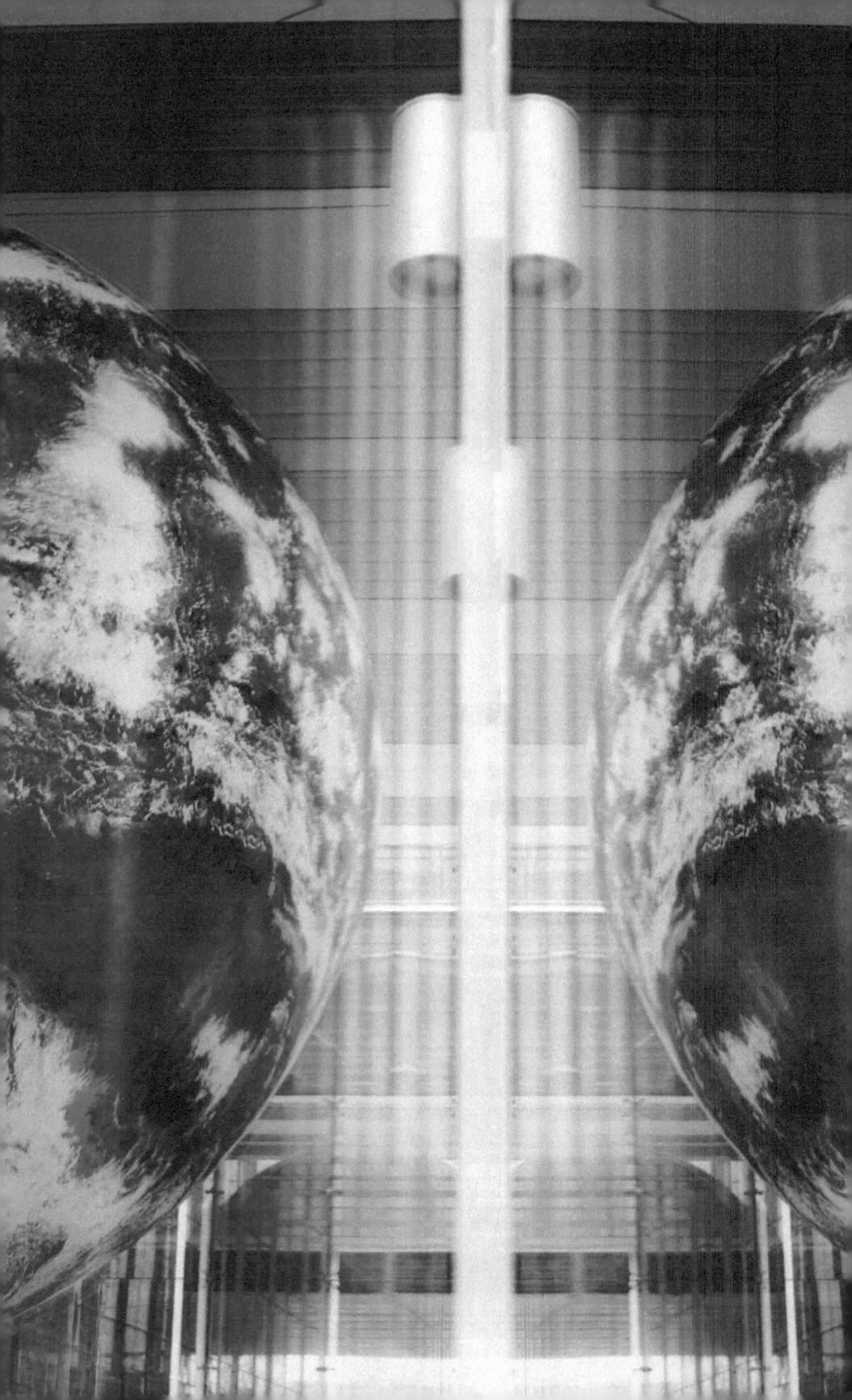

Crazy

I knew it, he said.
You writers are all crazy.
I wanted this to be a nightmare,
one that I'd wake from safe
and sound in his arms,
our bodies a perfect fit,
nearly the same temperature.
But my body was quick to overheat
and he liked to be covered in blankets.
That should have been my first clue.
Perhaps he wasn't nearly as aware
of his insecurities as I was.
Nearly—an adverb meaning
very close to, almost.
We were nearly a perfect fit
tangled legs in warm blankets.
Nearly—not perfect enough.
I still dream of him
I imagine those dreams as glimpses
of what nearly could have happened
if we had met in a different time
a different universe
a parallel one where maybe our
nearlys were perfects.

That Person

There will always be that one person
that when you hear his name,
on the lips of a friend,
that place you reserved in your heart for him—
that tiny space that will always be his
no matter who else comes after him,
whether there is one or none or hundreds—
that tiny space floats up, clinging to the
blood in your veins,
rushing
through your body,
into your mind.
And within seconds
images are flashing like forgotten dreams:

> Red jacket, soft smile, nervous.
> His hand resting on your hip under the blankets.
> Blue yoga pants separating his skin from yours.
> Waking up wrapped in his arms, hands entwined.
> Your head on his shoulder, TV tuned to *Jaws*.
> Early morning, his arm snaking over you to hit snooze.

And then your breath catches.
These are only memories now,
so then he settles back into that space
in your heart
sinking like a rock
tossed in the deepest river.

Safe

I found a poem I wrote
about the man before you.
In it, I told him
I felt safe with him.
And I remember telling you,
I wish you were here in my bed,
because I sleep better at your side.
Days later in the hall between
your bedroom and kitchen, you said,
Do you mean it?
As if you couldn't quite believe me.
The lights were dim and I couldn't
see your eyes, but I remember the smile.
I nodded, You make me feel safe.
After admitting that, it was
only a short time later that
you ended things.
A time in which I had felt like
I squeezed a pane of glass so hard it exploded.
It was a film noir landscape:
black and white
swirling, murky sky of your world
and a fuse lit by mine.
I realize now it was guilt
in the form of a question.
You never wanted to believe it,
that you could make someone
feel safe.

A Constellation of Questions

Some of these questions
I cannot fathom to comprehend.
Others I already know the answers to.
But it is there, in the hollow between them
that I lose myself.

These questions are a constant buzzing,
a quiet storm of words that
have never been spoken.

Yet they find their way to my lips
only to die in the air between us.

In Time

Teach me how to forget
that somewhere in time we are together,
and I'm curled up next to you in bed.
You, covered in the heavy brown blanket,
and I with the thin tan one.
Your face inches from mine, asking me
if I'm warm enough.

Teach me how to forget
that somewhere in time we are together
at your best friend's house
playing beer pong and I'm narrating
the match between you and your friends
and you laugh when I laugh
and that moment is perfect, to me.

Teach me how to forget
that somewhere in time we are together
and we're at McShea's before it turned into
Surfside and we're playing
Shut the Box and you lose
and you turn to me, grinning.
"See if you can get higher than 24."

Teach me how to forget
that somewhere in time we are together
and we're sitting across from
each other at Bluecoast, over a white
tablecloth. I ask you what kind of wine you'd like.
"Whatever you want, sweetheart."
Your blue shirt is neat, the tie fake.
"Whatever you pick out, I'll drink."

Teach me how to forget
that somewhere in time we are together.

My Hair Used To Be Long

My curls had grown quite a bit
since the last time your fingers swept
them from my neck, sweetly drawing me closer.

So I cut my hair.

I cut it short enough that I know
the hair remaining has never known
the feel of your fingers,
has never been tangled in passion.

I cut my hair to forget you
to forget the scent of you close to me
to forget the night you
kissed every inch of me,
under those iridescent stars.

And to forget that we tumbled to the floor,
wrapped in a blanket of secrecy,
murmuring secrets to each other.

The Air I Breathe

It's not that you don't want me,
that you're not interested
that makes me feel
like hellfire
is burning my insides.
It's that you can't even be
in the same room as me.
It's as if you can't even breathe
the same air that I'm breathing.

Winter Snow

My memory seemed timeless.
Each fiery thought targeted my
only feeling: love.

But love was like snow,
easily melted or blown away.
It had reached its end,
turning slushy
and gray,
like the streets after a plow.

747

Falling for someone is like descending from the sky in a 747
the tops of the clouds, soft and pure white, or fragile
and long and thick like cotton candy.
This is the surface, the outer shell, who you see
as you're standing next to him. As you go down,
the clouds change in texture,
lightning and rain and a smattering of hail and
these discolorations are learning that he likes hoppy beer
and that he orders his burger medium-well and
that he believes an omelet isn't a real omelet
unless it's made with at least six eggs. And he tells you
that the part of him that wants children wants
to adopt and you do, too. And then you descend deeper
and those fluffy, grey and white and thick and stormy clouds
part, begin to disappear, and suddenly you're seeing
things clearer; shapes and colors become cars and swimming pools.
You learn his sleep habits and that he believes his house
is too big for just him. You learn his favorite movies and music
and you realize that they nearly mimic yours: *Casablanca*, *Jaws*,
Fear & Loathing in Las Vegas, Ballyhoo, One Drop, Bob Marley,
and good old country like Johnny Cash and Merle Haggard.
And you learn that he likes oysters and goat cheese,
and Thai and Mexican, and you get closer and
cars grow larger, roads take shape and then it's all too clear
to you, that you have fallen for him, you've connected
to him and you smile more when he's around.
And the closer you get to the ground, the bigger things
seem so trivial. You realize that the clouds aren't so pure
and you don't want them to be. You want it all—the storms,
and lightning and thunder, the rain and snow.

You want traffic jams, dead-ends, mazes of highway.
And you wait to touch down into his darkest part.
And there is something about him that tells you: don't give up.
Only by the time you realize this, you have come to find that
he doesn't feel the same. And that's when the wheels touch tarmac
and he's not there anymore and you don't know where things went
wrong or what you did, but somewhere along the way

      he let go and you didn't.

Greek Therapy

I almost fell off a cliff
in Greece
Santorini, Megalochori, near the
Grandview Hotel.

And what a view it would have been
to be my last.

It didn't happen like in the movies.
There was no dramatic pause,
no slow motion.
It happened in real-time.
And it wasn't for lack of being careful,
but, like anything in life, it was unexpected.
I had paused on a ledge to photograph
a church perched on a volcanic island cliff.
I took a step onto the next ledge and before
my foot found purchase,
the boulder I had just stood on was rolling away,
down
down
it seemed like a hundred feet.
Rock and dirt tumbled
as I landed on one foot, and
gently placed the other next to it.
And then . . . there you were . . .
a mirage before my eyes. But you
        were really 5,201 miles away.

I used to spend hours, days, weeks
trying to tell you . . .
I still care.

Measures of Anger

The bitterness
had laced through me
like water over limestone.

In the twilight
of the last few months
I had never let my guard down,
never showed emotion.

But as I watched you,
your eyes finally closed,
I traced your features with mine.
Your lips, the curve of your brow,
careful not to stare too long
for fear you'd wake
and catch me.

Never had I felt so unguarded
and my measures of anger
shifted, changed into something else
secure, protected, safe.

Kintsugi
(golden joinery; to patch with gold)

The Japanese art philosophy that
repaired pieces of pottery or china,
should be aesthetically pleasing to the eyes,
fascinates me.

Kintsugi is the belief that broken
pieces are not meant to be covered or
mended so they look new.
The Japanese fit broken items back together
and then fill in the cracks and missing
parts with gold lacquer.
This beautifies the piece and gives it history;
its own story.

After you let me go, I broke
into hundreds of pieces.
I had told myself that I didn't need you
and I don't.
I'm happy without you.
But I want to have you in my life.
I want to share my happiness, my world,
with you.
So I let your laughter fill in the cracks you made.
And I let your smile build up the foundation
that you had crumbled.
And I let your wisdom and sarcasm find
voids to fill, to cement the pieces
of me back together.
And I see that those pieces, shining
with invisible gold
are because of you.
You are my Kintsugi.

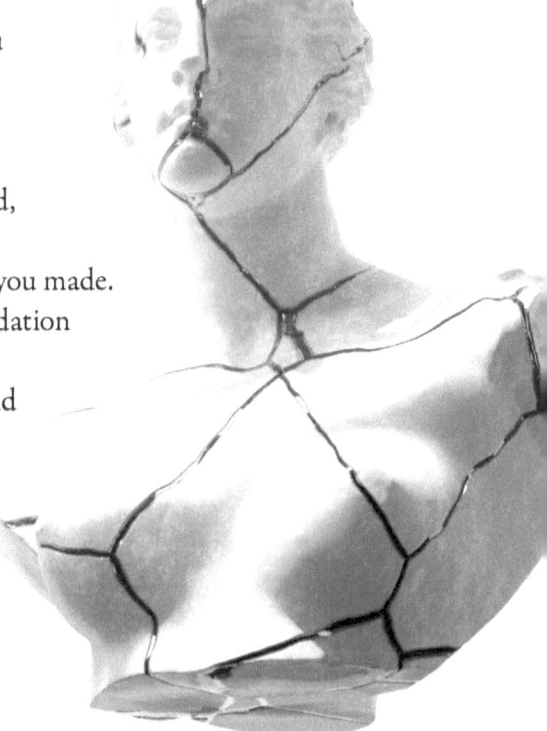

INTERLUDE

Light Year

*(a unit of astronomical distance equivalent to
the distance that light travels in one year)*

As a light year does not measure time,
I don't measure my time with you
I measure the distance.

When you are further away
that is when your light is brightest.

When you come closer to me,
the darkness sets in,
because your light grows small
and has traveled so far.

For example:
    Stars from the earth,
I know that they are massive—
    sometimes 100 times the size
of our own star—
but their light,
when it reaches us,
is but a speck in the inky sky.

So even when
your light draws nearer,
and I desperately want to hold on
to that beautiful light
you grow fainter
drowning in the larger picture.

I wonder, now
how you can measure the distance
of something you cannot grasp?

SUMMER

White Continent

Sunlight ripples over snow,
shadowing the land in red and gold.
The rays fan out
like the hair of scalloped mermaids
along the white sparkling tundra
of crystallized water.

I feel the heaviness of my decisions.
I feel trapped in a kingdom of ice.
Chambers and halls
surround me, but my hands, devoted
to making and shaping and molding
my life, do not move.
I close my eyes and feel the
closeness of the handle, the
door knob, but I cannot take it.
I cannot open it.

There are no roads here,
there are only halls
where the white blood cells have sealed
my cracks and make me airtight again,
strong enough
to hold until the next explosion of
ache and terror of square miles of destruction.

She is fragile, the halls say, she is a broken person.
She threw together the maybes of her life and
placed them in a jar,
as if she can fill the jar with hopes and wishes
and pixie dust.
As if they give wings to her maybes.

Origami Heart

I fold my heart,
crease, fold, crease, fold.
Like origami.
A swan,
to be specific, and I tuck it
in a little envelope, seal it with a
heart-shaped, signet antique ring,
in black wax.
And I watch as the mailman takes it away,
slips it into his bag, pats it gently,
as if he's keeping it safe for me.
Perhaps it will disappear into the blue,
never to be seen or read again, like some mail.
Or maybe it will come back years from now, when
I have given up. See, I have
mailed it to myself for safekeeping, a kind of
poor man's copyright.
I am waiting for someone who knows how to
break the seal, open the envelope and
take out the little
origami swan and unfold it and
keep it safe, like the frayed remnants
of a tie that my aunt kept in a
wooden box; the unforgotten, ash-covered tie
that floated into her backyard
from Ground Zero.
I am looking for someone to keep
my origami heart in a box.

Photograph

I take photographs because
years from now I will want to remember
the events that shaped my life.
I will want to recall trips overseas.
I will want to remember where I have been
and what I have accomplished
and I can easily pull up these images
and sync my memories to colors
and sights
and eventually those
photographs
will give way to the smells and sounds
and textures of the moments in my head
and those sensations will begin to
spread through and over my body
as if I were right back there again.

But I never
took photos of any of you.
And I realized, I don't need them
as your memories will forever
be locked into my mind,
as if etched by the universe.
I won't need a photograph of you
to remember the way you made me
feel and the words you spoke to me
or how your fingers seemed to be
magic on my body.

All of you shaped who I am
and what I have become
and the peace I have found.

She

She will be vulnerable,
but that means she does not
fear her emotions.
She will feel them,
allow them to pass through her.

She will write about them.
Some of them may be
about you.
And they may or may not be kind.

Don't think that because
you are in one of these pieces,
that shows a different side of you,
that her feelings have changed.

She knows that you cannot fully love
someone until you have seen
their darkness.

I Hope You Can Heal

I hope you can learn to forgive
yourself and others.

I hope you can begin to see that
bottling up emotions serves no purpose.

I hope you can learn to express yourself
through your writing, love.

I hope you can put to paper
the heartaches
and failures
and struggles you have
dwelling deep inside you.

I hope you can exorcise
the demons in your head because
you are wonderful
and you deserve love.

Buried

I buried my feelings,
the ones I have for you.
I forced them down under
miniscule grains of sand and shells
along every beach I walked on this summer—
from Delaware to Ocean City.

I thought they were safe,
buried like treasure,
washed by the ocean several times a day:
at night and under the sun.

But even after fleeing
to a beach on the other side
of the planet,
my feelings found me.

They rose up, seemingly
out of the clear, blue Mediterranean.
They crawled out of the ocean,
up on the shore like the spirits of
dead pirates and mingled
with the shells and pebbles
on a beach in Mykonos.

I buried them again,
and walked back up the cliffside,
back to the safety of the villa.

And yet again my feelings rose up
but this time it wasn't on a beach.
It was on the side of a volcano,
along a trail, hundreds of feet above
that same Mediterranean sea.
These feelings must have
traveled through the land, rushing
like the lava beneath, with speed,
forcing a boulder to give way,
rocks and stones scurrying down
the cliff after it, begging for it to come
back up and put itself right, to
force the lava-feelings back into the earth.

But it didn't
and I finally understood:
sometimes
feelings just need to stay.

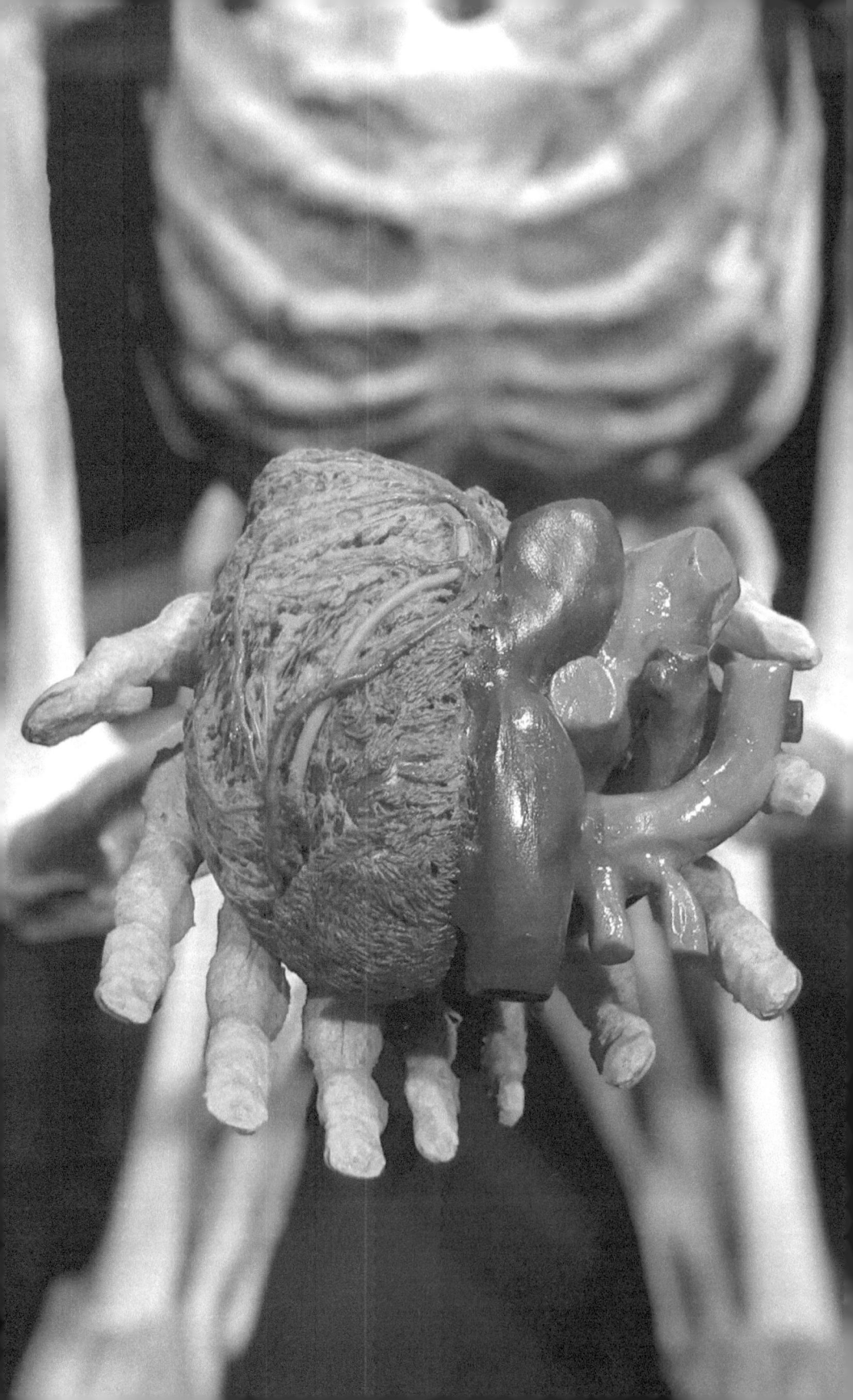

One Job, Dear Heart

You have one job Heart.
Just one: my blood.
To make sure it flows smoothly
and fastidiously through my veins.
Your job is to get oxygen to
every part of my body.
My brain, legs, fingers, and toes.
Your job is to send the used blood
through the right atrium, through the
tricuspid valve and into the right
ventricle, then into the lungs,
leaving behind carbon dioxide,
then re-oxygenating my blood.

You're not supposed to
wonder what it's like to feel someone's lips on mine.
It's not your job to beat faster
when they're around or when they say my name.

> I know my name.
> Don't make me excited to hear it
> upon the lips of someone who
>   doesn't want me.

Your job is to send oxygen-rich blood from
my lungs, from my pulmonary veins into my heart,
through the left atrium and out the aorta valve.
Your job is to oxygenate my body.
Your job is not to send a rush of blood to
my head, making my emotions swirl and
my mind long for him. And
it's certainly not meant to skip beats
when that person's skin touches mine.
You have one job, Heart,
and that is to keep me alive.

Pendulum

My heart swings as if it were
a pendulum:
North to South, happy to sad.
East to West, turmoil to pain.

   Northeast
sweet torment.
   Southwest
painful heaviness.
   Southeast
physical sadness.
   Northwest
bittersweet, that happy pain,
of remembering how good
things could have been.

I wish my pendulum heart
would stop swinging
for just a moment.

What I Learned In Greece

I learned that the air is sweeter
and the feeling it leaves on your skin
is like kisses from a lover.

I learned that the water is saltier,
clearer, and the sand coats your body
in a layer of armor only the sea can break.

I learned that the sun is hotter,
and it tans you a different color, making you
feel like you've been to a different planet.

I learned that sleep is optional, and so
is drinking, but if you drink until six a.m.,
spinach pie at a Greek bakery is a must.

I learned that salads are best with real
Greek cheese and lemon juice on fried
potatoes is the only way to eat them.

I learned that hiking from Fira to Oia
is mandatory just for the views
and that Ouzo is pure Greek medicine.

I learned that Santorini is not just
magical to see, but that it creates magic
long after you've left.

I learned on the ferry from Santorini to Paros,
that the past is a precursor to better things.
That I didn't need a map.

I learned that I needed to get
incredibly fucking lost
so that I could my way again.

Ocean Power

There's learning power in things
you cannot control.

I stumbled out of the ocean,
knelt in the sand,
coughing and spitting saltwater
from my lungs.

This was power, I thought.
She's the meanest thing
on the planet—the ocean—and
if you're not careful
she could tear you apart.

Writers

I believe writers feel life more than most.
Their heart breaks a thousand times over
after one lost love.

When they love and lose, they do so
every single day, because memories
never die.

Writers have a knack for
memorizing the smallest of details.
They remember every nuance
of voice.

They remember
every inhale,
and exhale,
and kiss,
and touch,
and freckle,
and laugh,
and every time a laugh
is absent.

They remember whispered words
and scents
as clearly as the sun
remembers flowers.

My Mind Was Still Angry

It churned.
I wanted nothing more than to snap but
that's not who I am, instead
I held it together long enough
to make it to the ocean.
I held it together through red lights,
through blaring horns,
through traffic that wouldn't move.
I held it together as I apologized for something
that had nothing to do with me.
I drove,
barely keeping my speed in check,
barely stopping at stop signs.
I had to get there.
I parked and ran to the beach.
My solace, my sanctuary
is that beautiful salty water.

I dropped my bag and
ran into the ocean.

That's when I lost it.
That's when the tears flowed.
That's when eight hours of holding it together,
and pent-up, swirling emotions
released from my body.
I cried. I heaved. I gasped. I tasted salt.
I let my tears mix with the sea.
And it's not sadness—
I cry when I'm angry.

So I let the tears flow.
I let the ocean, in her wonder, float my body,
hold me in her embrace.
It was almost as if she felt
my anger,
her waves swelled, pulling me
out,
lifting me
up.
The waves grew
and she was there.
She took my body,
reeling in rage, and responded in kind.
But just to show that she was comforting me.
That it was okay to let go.

Let me do this for you, she said.
Let me take your tears and body and heal you.
Let me be angry for you.
My body insists on crying when I really
just want to spit nails.
But as long as the ocean is here,
I'll never be angry alone.

EPILOGUE

Moments

Lately I've been into moments,
capturing them in my memory.
Their nuances—
the sounds, smells, tastes, touches
and the reasons they affect me.

I've seen the world from the top of a cliff,
looking down into water forty feet deep,
seeing rocks with sharp edges and
a part of me wanted to step back, but
I didn't.

You see, this part of me, this little voice
in my head needed this more than
the part of me that actually wanted to jump.

I don't remember holding my breath
or even that first thought as I fell,
but I held that moment in my mind.

I have sometimes dreamt of that leap
in the weeks and months since,
a moment of pure exhilaration.

It was like falling in love.
You don't even know it's happening
until you're in the water,
until you're treading and tasting salt
on your lips.
Salt
or tears.

Thank You

I am so grateful to all the friends and family who have lent me support in my journey to rediscover my soul and spirit in love. Thank you for letting me cry on your shoulder—through email and messaging or in real life.

I am grateful to the Universe for all the inspiration It has sent my way. I could not have written what I have here without feeling the magic of nature and science and spirituality to my very core and allowing it to change me as a person and as a lover.

To my "Greek" family: you know who you are; you are all inspiring and I love every one of you as deeply as the Aegean Sea. Thank you especially to Dimitra for forcing me to go to Greece a second time even when I changed my mind. The skinny dipping on that Mykonos beach will forever be etched in my soul. Liberating.

A special thanks to Amy Bertrand Mullins for being my rock and sounding board in all this.

To Samantha, your advice is priceless—I adore you.

To Gail Braune Comorant and Ethan Joella for reading a few poems each and giving me feedback: it's much appreciated and greatly valued.

To Ellen Collins for the most thorough of edits three years later. I am in awe of your poetic surgery. Namaste.

And last but not least, to those men: thank you.

ABOUT CRYSTAL

Crystal Heidel is the owner of Byzantium Sky Press, an indie traditional publishing company located in Ellendale, Delaware. She also owns Heimat Publishing, a service-based publishing company that allows self-publishing authors to enlist her award-winning expertise in cover design.

She is the author of the NFPW First Place Award-Winning, Delaware-set, 5-star murder mystery, *Still Life in Blood*. She currently is working on *Still Life in Ice*, and an untitled science fiction novel in addition to plotting the third *Still Life* book.

She divides her free time between writing, reading, sharpening her cooking skills, and spending time with family and friends. She likes to observe award-winning movies and successful television shows for the conciseness of dialogue and the use of smash cuts and lighting to try to create near-perfect scenes in her own writing.

She's a member of the Rehoboth Beach Writers' Guild and a long-time resident of Sussex County, Delaware. She loves to practice yoga, walk the local trails, workout in her home gym, and travels often—from Pennsylvania and Maryland, to New York and Virginia, as well as worldwide.

You can email Crystal at byzantiumskypress@gmail.com.

www.ingramcontent.com/pod-product-compliance
Lightning Source LLC
Chambersburg PA
CBHW030223140626
46545CB00012B/2966